The Mindset Makeover

Living Your Life with Clarity and Purpose

By

Wendie Lloyd

Copyright © Wendie Lloyd
9820 Northcross Center Court Suite 157
Huntersville, NC 28078
704-746-8331
Coachingwhatmatters@gmail.com

Table of Contents

Introduction 1

Chapter 1: Ignite Your Purpose 3

Chapter 2: Be Still 16

Chapter 3: Grateful Mind - Grateful Heart 27

Chapter 4: Embrace Your Obstacles 38

Chapter 5: Fearful to Fearless 52

Chapter 6: Forgiveness 61

Chapter 7: Relationships 75

Bringing it all Together 84

Dedication

First and foremost, it is with tremendous gratitude that I dedicate this book to God, who made this possible. My two sons, who are the greatest blessings in my life. My parents, who are both deceased, but set the foundation for who I am today. My family, who has always supported, encouraged, and stood by my side. My amazing friends that have been there with me through the laughter and tears. All my clients who have entrusted me with their deepest secrets, thoughts, emotions, and fears and allowed me to join them along their journey. My mentors, teachers, colleagues, and coaches who have given me insight and encouragement. And to those who have taught me some of life's toughest lessons of disappointment, hurt, and pain. These relationships and trials have yielded the most growth.

Introduction

For several years, people have been telling me that I need to write a book and share my experiences and knowledge. I avoided the task for various reasons, one of which was deciding what to write about. I knew that my primary goal for writing a book would be to help others live with gratitude, fulfillment, and abundance.

As time has passed, I grew both personally and professionally, which led me to a life changing revelation. I learned that the most valuable asset we possess is our mindset. The mind is connected to all other aspects of our lives. Thoughts, perceptions, behaviors, emotions and even our health are ultimately controlled by the mind. From this transformative truth, came the title of my book, "The Mindset Makeover." The intention of this book is to assist you with changing your mindset and aligning your purpose, perspective, and priorities to attain your goals and live a purpose filled life.

We may not be able to control our circumstances, relationships, or environments, but we can control our mindset and perceptions. As a counselor and coach, I've discovered that the biggest difference between those who move beyond their obstacles and those who remain stuck is their ability to transform their mindset.

We are equipped to consistently learn and grow with a purpose. When we become stagnant, we stop living the life we are created to live. Our mind, heart, body and soul are intricately connected, which means that a shift malfunction in one impacts our entire being. Think of your mind as the control center. Throughout this book, you will read about various life experiences and the role mindset played in the outcomes. You will learn practical applications that will help you make sustainable changes to your mindset.

Life is filled with challenges, traumas, losses and disappointments, but we have the power within to tackle these obstacles and live a fulfilled life. You are able to choose the way you want to live your life. My hope is for you is to see that even though your journey may have some difficulties, you can laugh, learn, and love along the way.

Chapter 1
Ignite Your Purpose

"You were put on this earth to achieve your greatest self, to live out your purpose, and to do it courageously."
~Steve Maraboli~

It was a hot July day in Southern Illinois. My college boyfriend and I had just returned from a whitewater rafting trip in West Virginia. We were hungry, exhausted from the long drive, and needed showers. While his mom was preparing dinner for us, I was getting my things together to take a shower, when my dad called. This was unusual since it was always my mom who would initiate the phone calls. Although he was trying to stay calm, I could hear anxiety in his voice. He and my mom had to return early from their trip because my mom had become ill and was in the ICU at the hospital in my hometown. The heaviness of dread and fear overcame me. I quickly packed my car, and due to the drive being close to four hours and my emotional state, my boyfriend's parents had him drive me home.

We went directly to the hospital and when I saw my mom laying in the hospital bed with a breathing tube down her throat, I felt as if I had been punched in the gut. I knew I wanted to be strong and not break down in front of her. As I walked closer, she reached for my hand, and I could see the tears in her eyes. She looked sad. Since she couldn't talk, she had a board that she wrote on to communicate with us. She wrote, "I love you," on the board and squeezed my hand. I was overcome with emotions at the realization that she was close to the end of her life. She was my best friend. I am the youngest of six with a significant age gap between me and my siblings, which meant that during my childhood, she had more time available to spend with me.

It wasn't long after this moment that I was sitting by a pond near my home with my nephew. He looked at me and said, "I wonder if Grandma is happy now." In almost an instant after he uttered those words, the hospital called. On my way to the hospital, I dropped my nephew off at my neighbor's house. Once the car door shut behind him, an immediate rush of tears flooded my cheeks. My mom was gone.

As you embrace the journey of life, it is crucial to remember that you were created for a purpose. Life truly is short, and we never know when our time is up. So, it's important to define and live your life with purpose. A clear definition of your purpose and a positive mindset gives direction, meaning, and focus to your journey. The right mindset creates sustainable growth and change that will keep you on course to a fulfilling and abundant life. A life without purpose is like a hamster running on his wheel, constantly in motion but going nowhere.

While on a recent beach trip, I stopped in a small local restaurant for a quick burger. As I've learned when traveling, go where the locals go. It's often the best food. While sitting at the bar waiting on my food, a tall gray-haired gentleman walked up, sat next me, and introduced himself as Tom. Tom and I began talking, and he shared that he had recently retired from coaching high school sports and bought a small place at the beach. After about six months, he realized his dream of retiring to the beach wasn't all he thought it would be. At first, he developed an effective daily routine, but after years of teaching and coaching, he found that life had become boring. The following day, Tom was heading back home for an interview with a small college for a coaching position, but he really didn't think returning to full time coaching was his answer.

Tom was at a transition point in his life. Up until that point, his life had been fulfilling. Of course, it wasn't always perfect, and he had his struggles. He went through two divorces as well as other obstacles, but overall, he believed he had a rewarding life thus far. Coaching gave Tom purpose. He knew that this was his calling because at one point, he had left his coaching job for a banking job. It wasn't long before he realized his heart was connected to coaching. He returned to the school and position he left.

Tom's life had purpose while coaching, but once he retired, he felt lost. He lost his sense of direction and focus. Although he was considering returning to coaching, he knew that this really wasn't the right direction for this stage in his life. He needed to redefine his purpose and reframe his mindset to feel that sense of fulfillment again.

Tom's story demonstrates a few important characteristics of purpose. The first is that even though you may experience hard times, if your life has purpose, you will feel fulfilled. Also, as you grow and hit key pivotal transitional points in life, your purpose may change. There may be a need for refinement or a shift of perspective in regards to that purpose. While coaching, Tom felt joy and clarity in his life. Once that purpose was fulfilled and his course changed, he was discontent. He was living out his dream, but it had become void of passion.

Over the years in my counseling practice, I've treated numerous people struggling with depression, anxiety, or overall dissatisfaction. I have realized that the commonality between them was a lack of purpose. It gives life meaning and direction. Without purpose, there may be a feeling of hopelessness or discontentment. I would help them with coping mechanisms and skills to manage their symptoms. We would explore their past and current relationships along with life experiences. However, I found that the most productive and sustainable outcomes came from helping these individuals discover their purpose.

Discovering and clearly defining your unique purpose is the key to living an enriching life. We are all unique and our definitions may vary. For some of us, the definition seems simple and yet for others, it's more complex. Defining your purpose is unique to you. You may believe your purpose is to serve God, but HOW are you going to do that? Some may find their purpose is working with children or helping the elderly. Others may find their purpose in running a Fortune 500 company or running their own company. Some may believe it is finding the cure for cancer or fighting for human rights.

You must paint the picture. How do you see yourself living out your purpose? Being specific and clear will help simplify your life. There will be times that you may need to refine or even redefine it. The key is to be specific and have a vivid understanding of your unique definition.

We receive hope by formulating a plan of where we are headed and why. It gives us the strength to endure the obstacles and gives us a positive focus. When we have something to work towards, it gives us a reason to get out of bed in the morning. One of the first things I do with my coaching clients is help them clearly define their purpose and what success means to them. This sets the foundation for a successful coaching journey with my clients. It creates a foundation for them to grow and sustain change and success. A clear sense of purpose adds meaning to life.

Do you remember the specifics from your childhood? What did you dream about becoming when you grew up? My dreams varied throughout my childhood, but as a young child, I remember wanting to be a mom. My friends and I played house for hours. We had a set up in our basement with a play kitchen and we would take turns being the mom, child, dad, sister or whoever fit in the family at the time. At one point, I thought being an administrative assistant, or secretary as we knew them, would be fun.

I was looking for my path, my direction, and my purpose. As children, our imagination takes us on a journey until we eventually end up where we want to be. As we continue to grow, our dreams can become cloudy or seem unattainable. We may lose sight of our direction. For some of us, our dreams don't change but for others, they may drastically change.

Discovering your purpose is a process and requires self-exploration. Identifying all the aspects of who you are is significant in the process. Throughout your life, you play various roles. Picture a circle divided up into the various pieces that define your life: family, social, professional, spiritual, health/fitness, educational, financial, leisure, etc. Then, imagine the pieces divided according to the actual time and energy spent in each area. Are the pieces divided equally? If the answer is yes, then you are in the extreme minority.

More often, the size of the pieces varies, and people are frequently amazed when looking at the reality of where they are investing their time and energy. Now, create your ideal circle, dividing the pieces according to how you would like them to be. This will help you gain perspective of where you are and where you wish to be. This will help you create a path with an end goal in sight.

Bill was a forty-eight-year-old successful business executive. Married for over 20 years, he enjoyed a healthy and fulfilling relationship with his wife. Not only that, his relationships with his son, parents, and extended family were great as well. Bill was satisfied with his spiritual life and was financially secure. He came to me for coaching because he knew something was out of sync in his life.

Professionally, he was working at his "perfect" job. He determined this based on an assessment he had taken years earlier that indicated the type of profession he was meant to be in. However, after a promotion in his "ideal" job, he felt a void. On workdays, Bill found it increasingly more difficult to get up in morning, and his agitation with his employees was becoming problematic.

Based on the assessment, he set and attained a goal, which made it seem like he had achieved his dream job, but in reality, he didn't feel the passion. The reason for this was he wasn't really living out his purpose.

After working together, Bill did some self-exploration and realized he was spending much more time and energy at his job then he wanted. His "aha" moment came when he realized his job wasn't fulfilling his purpose or creating passion. The good news is through further exploration and guidance, he was able to define his purpose.

Together, we were able to outline a plan for Bill to align his professional life with his passion. He was able to find a way to provide financially for his family while feeling passionate about his professional life. The rest of our time focused on shifting his mindset, so he could live out his purpose. Currently, Bill reports increased appreciation for his marriage and family, which he realized wasn't as satisfying as he had previously assumed. He feels more connected spiritually and has increased his satisfaction with his career. He no longer feels stuck or dreads getting up in the morning, and his overall motivation has increased and sustained.

When we are living out our purpose, we create a deep passion inside and life becomes more satisfying. A purposeful life breeds increased motivation and fulfillment. Discovering this is like a light bulb going off in your mind. It is the "aha" moment that lights a fire within.

This chapter is about igniting your purpose that will become a burning fire within. Passion and purpose are closely connected. According to the "The Purpose Driven Life," by Rick Warren, "Purpose always produces passion. Nothing energizes like a clear purpose." What gets you excited? What stirs up your emotions? When you're passionate about something, you have an intense level of emotional energy. Have you ever been in love? You feel butterflies in your stomach, you wake up with a smile, and life seems to have more meaning and purpose. Equally motivating can be something that has caused you pain or anger. Those emotions can create a passion for change. Sometimes it's our passion that helps us find our purpose. Once we have a sense of purpose though, our passion is fully ignited.

Candy Lighter founded Mothers Against Drunk Drivers (MADD) in the early 1980's after her daughter was killed by a drunk driver. She took the passion caused by her pain and anger to create a purpose for her life. In the midst of her deepest pain, she was able to funnel her energy in a purposeful way to prevent others from having to suffer the same type of loss she had to bear. This is an example of how our passion can propel us to discover our purpose. In the following chapters, I will expand further upon how to take the energy from a tragedy and direct it towards a positive flow for the use of your purpose.

Living your life with purpose gives you direction, a foundation, and passion. A life filled with gratitude and optimism is easier when we are living with intent. For some of us, your purpose may change as you experience life or may find it becomes clearer as you grow. Others may discover their purpose at a young age and maintain that throughout their life.

In the midst of writing this book, the Las Vegas mass shooting occurred. As I sat listening to the interviews of the victims on the NBC network, one story in particular stood out. A twenty-one-year-old young man was describing the event from his perspective, and he talked about the blood on his shirt. He was unsure of where it came from and he described the immense fear he and his sister felt. One minute they were listening to country music and without warning, they were running for their lives. He stated that up until this event, he was Agnostic. After his experience, he started believing in God because he realized his need for hope and a sense of purpose. During the deepest, darkest moment of this young man's life, he realized that his life needed purpose and meaning.

Another story of finding purpose out of this tragedy is from the country music artist, Eric Church. Eric was one of the headliners at the Route 91 Harvest Music Festival. The following week, he was scheduled to perform at the Grand Ole Opry. A video was released on YouTube featuring his performance. In the video, he explained how after the tragedy, he didn't want to perform at the venue. However, prior to the event, someone had sent him a video from an interview on CNN. A lady whose husband had been killed while saving her life on that horrific night in Las Vegas explained that they were at the festival to see Eric Church. She also said they had tickets to see his performance at the Grand Ole Opry as well.

After watching this video, Eric now agreed to perform. Inspired by the interview, he wrote a song in honor of this man's life and the others that were killed. He explained that his music was what carried him through the difficult times. He found purpose in performing that night. Using the power of his passion for music, he provided strength to the survivors, honored the victims, and found his own motivation to continue in spite of this horrific tragedy.

Several years ago, I went through the process of a divorce. After twenty years of marriage and two sons, my life was completely changed almost overnight. Throughout the process, there were varying degrees of emotions, sleepless nights, and endless days. As anyone who has experienced divorce may attest to, it is a grief process and can be a time of deep inner reflection.

In the midst of this process, I woke up one morning and said to myself, "You can continue to live in the past and be a victim, or you can make a change and defy the lies that have been fed to you. You can become who you were created to be." In that moment, it occurred to me that I needed to create a business that would help others going through transitions such as divorce, empty nest, career change, or any other major life shift. I realized I could use my personal experience as well as my professional training to help others beyond the realm of psychotherapy. Coaching What Matters LLC was created shortly thereafter. The name has significance for my path, which is to help others in whatever matters most in their lives. Coaching What Matters gave me a purpose to move past my divorce and create something positive out of the trauma.

Realizing your need for purpose and then defining it is a great start to living your life with intent and achieving abundance. Being able to gain vision and clarity to actually live your purposeful life is the next step. Remember your value when defining your purpose. Your time, energy and experiences are priceless so make sure to funnel them into a purposeful way of living. Learning to live your life with purpose doesn't mean you will be free from obstacles or pain, but it does mean that you will experience more joy and ability to handle struggles in a healthy way.

Getting your mindset in alignment with your values and beliefs will allow you to embrace this new way of living. Your mindset is the key to sustaining a life of purpose, clarity, and abundance. When you discover your purpose and begin applying it to your life, the days will be more enjoyable, and work becomes less stressful. Life has a richer meaning and each accomplished task brings you closer to the vision for your life.

Chapter 2
Be Still

"Wisdom comes once we learn to become still; in the silence of the heart and mind one learns his journey."
~Unknown~

Living life with purpose and clarity requires feeling centered and grounded. In order for our mindset to be focused and positive, we need to minimize all distractions. Our mindset can be much like a computer. As your computer accumulates files, it begins to process slower. To restore proper speed, you must move things to Dropbox, iCloud, or a flash drive. As you clean it out, it begins to operate more efficiently.

Multiple studies concluded that humans have an average of 50,000 – 70,000 thoughts per day. There are 86,4000 seconds in one day, which means we have just under one thought every second. Of those thoughts, it's estimated that 95% are recurring thoughts. Additionally, 70-80% of those thoughts are negative. These staggering numbers reveal the overwhelming amount of processing that goes on in our heads. At the same time, the majority of these thoughts are repetitive and negative. Like the computer, information overload can lead to excessive distractions when our mind is busy processing all these thoughts. Even more difficult is when a traumatic event occurs or we need to make a major decision.

Getting yourself grounded and focused to be still and listen takes conscious effort. As a society, we have become so connected to our cell phones and instant contact that it has become an expectation. People often become frustrated when someone doesn't respond instantly. To avoid this damaging trend, take time to disengage from all distractions. Turn off the phone, computer, and television. Take a walk, go for a run, sit by the ocean, go for a drive in the mountains, or take a hike in the woods. Get away from the daily stressors and noise.

Visualization is a great tool to help with focus and grounding. I've discovered that when I tell my clients to visualize a place that is relaxing, safe, and peaceful, the majority of them imagine an ocean or some type of water. Some of my clients also imagine some other form of nature. Visualizing these environments can rid your mind of all the clutter that may be present. Physically experiencing these environments can be helpful as well.

Many vacations are taken near water, lakes, the ocean, or resorts with swimming pools. If you've ever sat next to a waterfall, you know the calming impact. Water is a symbol of renewal and salvation in Christianity and many spiritual cultures. In Chinese medicine, water is seen as necessary for harmony and balance. Therefore, when looking to get grounded and focused, water is a great resource. Soaking in a warm bath or taking a shower can be a relaxing option after a long, stressful day.

I go to the ocean when I begin to feel overwhelmed or distracted. If I'm struggling to make a big decision or feel unsettled, the ocean is my therapy. In Wallace Nicoles's book, "Blue Mind," he discusses the impact the ocean has on our mind. He defines the "blue mind" as a mildly meditative state characterized by calm, peacefulness, unity, and a sense of general happiness and satisfaction with life in the moment. He further discusses the ocean having a meditative effect. The sound, the motion of the waves, and even the color of the water creates a state of focus and calm. When you're in a grounded, calm state, your mind slows down. Thoughts become clearer and stressful energy dissipates.

This is why so many people choose a beach as their vacation destination. Some of my best night sleeps have been in an oceanfront room with the door open, listening to the ocean's waves hit the shore and feeling the breeze of the salty air. A morning run, reflective time sitting on the beach, and feeling the sand beneath my feet help me feel grounded and connected to my soul. The ocean is where I feel the most connected to God. This where I have some of my best conversations with God. My heart and mind are filled with awe and gratitude. Wallace Nicoles's research validates that the ocean has similar impact on the majority of people.

When our mind is in a calm state, it's easier to think clearly. In chapter one, I discussed the importance of igniting your purpose. If you are struggling with this or need clarity in your life, the ocean is a great place to escape. What if you can't get to the ocean? There are sound machines, phone apps, YouTube videos, and many other resources that provide ocean sounds. While listening to the sound of the waves, close your eyes. Imagine yourself sitting in front of the ocean, the blue sky above, the waves coming in and going out, the smell of salty air, a warm breeze, and soft sand below your feet. Allow the image and sound to relax your mind. As you see the waves go out, visualize all your stress, anxiety, and fears going out with the waves. As the waves come in, inhale the positive renewed energy.

As your mind calms and thoughts become clear, ask yourself questions, and then listen for the answers. Whether you believe the answers are coming from your soul, your heart, your mind, God, or the universe; if your quiet and listen, you'll begin to hear the answers. If you aren't hearing the answers, allow your mind to just be calm. Sometimes the answers come later or in other ways. The key is being still and letting thoughts flow without attempting to control, justify, or question them.

Your mind is like the engine in a car. It needs to be taken care of and maintained to function. If the engine isn't working efficiently, the car won't operate properly. It's even worse if the engine dies because then the car loses its purpose. Proper maintenance entails taking care of the motor before it needs repair or breaks down. You need to change the oil on a regular basis, replace the fluids periodically, change the air filter, and use proper fuel for optimum functioning. Your mind is similar. Intentional, consistent care allows your body to properly function. Positive thoughts will flow freely, you will have the ability to actually feel your emotions, and most importantly, you will discover and live your purpose. In order to have clear thoughts, you need to clear out the negative chatter, let go of past hurts, and gain awareness of what you're allowing to enter and remain in your mind.

Your mind needs daily maintenance to function clearly. Remember, everyday you are processing a large number of thoughts. The mind is the command center of your heart, soul and body. It is the driving force of your thoughts, decisions, perceptions, and motivation. Awareness and care must be a priority. If you don't take care of your mind, you'll feel stressed, unfocused, and your ability to rationalize may be compromised. Making decisions is more difficult when your mind is constantly in motion.

I'm sure you've experienced this before. You oversleep for work, a scheduled flight, or any other important event. After a few choice words, you jump up and rush around getting ready. How do you feel in this moment? What do you feel for the next couple of hours or the rest of the day? If you are like most people, this one mistake sets the tone for your day. Unless you learn how to calm your mind, you will feel rushed and unsettled throughout the day. There are various practices you can use to calm your mind, gain clarity and regain composure to maintain peace throughout the rest of your day. First of all, remember that your mind, body, heart and soul are all connected; therefore, caring for one means that you are caring for the whole. If your mind is the command center, it makes sense to begin caring for your mind first and the rest will be easier to maintain.

Being still is a practice that must be a part of your daily routine. Beginning and ending your day with some quiet time allows your mind to focus and remove any negative energy. Ending the day with quiet time allows you to release the energy from the day and let go of any negative thoughts.

It gives you time to clear your mind, which allows for restful sleep.

Starting your day by priming your mind, is one practice that is used by some of the most successful people. Before starting a lawn mower, you often have to prime the engine. Priming an engine is the process of getting the fuel flowing to the motor. Similarly, priming your mind at the beginning of the day allows positive thoughts to begin flowing. It sets the tone for the day, allows your focus to flow in a positive direction, and sets your mind in a healthy frame.

Priming your mind starts with positive focus in a quiet setting. The following list presents an effective method of priming your mind as your day begins. This process can take anywhere from 10 minutes to 30 minutes. It's worth waking up a few minutes earlier to begin your day with a positive mindset.

- Begin with focused breathing. Breathe in through your nose and out through your mouth. Make sure to take a deep breath in and truly exhale from down in your gut to release all the negative energy.

- Spend time in gratitude prayer or meditation.

- Reflect on a positive thought, Bible verse, song lyric or other type of positive reflection

- Visualize your day as you would like it to unfold

- Look in the mirror and make a positive proclamation! (i.e. Today, I'm going to rock that presentation!)

- Engage in some form of physical activity to get your body moving

- Turn on some motivational, upbeat music and continue on with your day

Priming your mind is also an effective tool whenever you need focus. Many athletes have a routine for getting in the zone or priming before every game. My son has a routine of priming when he participates in a motorsports event. He has explained the strategies he uses for focusing before he goes out on the racetrack. Once he gets in his car and puts on his helmet, he focuses on the sound of the motor, the smell of the rubber, and envisions the track and racing to and taking the checkered flag. He eliminates all distractions and focuses completely on the race in front of him and his goal of taking the checkered flag.

Additionally, various types of exercises and physical movement can also prove effective with centering and calming your mind. Yoga is one form used to aid in mental focus and awareness. There are many forms of yoga. If this is something you'd like to incorporate in your life, research which type of yoga is best suited for you. Tai Chi, stretching, running and walking are also forms of exercise that are equally as effective in helping with clarity and focus.

Several years ago, I experienced many overwhelming events within a short period of time. While going through a stressful divorce, I experienced an early onset and an accelerated completion of menopause. I also had a significant shift in my thyroid function and a transition in my business all while raising my youngest son, who was a senior in high school and active in baseball. During a check-up with my doctor, she told me I needed to find a release for my stress before it affected my health even more significantly than it already had. I had already begun doing Pilates but decided to try running. Up until that point, I had not been a runner. Growing up, I actually avoided it at all costs. I followed a program a friend suggested, which was running on a treadmill and gradually increasing the distance and speed to three miles and up.

Once I graduated to running outside, I realized the true benefits. It became my way to relieve stress but also helped to clear my mind. Just as sitting by the ocean, many times some of my best ideas have come during and following a run. My stress levels reduce, and my mind becomes clear. Many runners express similar sentiments.

Music can be another mode of getting still and centered. Listening to calming music has been proven to increase focus and alter mood. As found in an article from 2015 in "Psychology Today," there has been an abundance of research on music and Attention Deficit Hyperactivity Disorder (ADHD). The research shows a significant increase in focus of people who have been diagnosed with ADHD in conjunction with music. It has been discovered that there are low levels of dopamine, a neurotransmitter which essentially transmits signals between nerve cells of the brain. The full explanation is beyond the scope of this book but mentioned to explain the benefit of music. This is why many doctors prescribed a stimulant to help increase focus for ADHD, a stimulant increases dopamine.

A study by Valerie Salimpoor and colleagues conducted in 2011, shows that music increases dopamine, the same effect of the stimulants. Studies have also shown that students with ADHD have improved test scores when listening to music while taking a test. The best types of music for the purpose of increased focused and centering, are those without lyrics, classical or nature sounds. Music is a great medium for our minds and souls. Integrating it into your life also decreases stress and adds enjoyment.

Being still and grounded is an essential practice for the health of your mind. Clearing out the built up and daily chatter helps you to gain focus, clarity and release stress. When you are looking for life answers, preparing goals, defining or refining your purpose or feeling overwhelmed: find a way to be quiet and still and listen. Whether it's time in nature, exercise, music, or closing your eyes and visualizing a peaceful place, get in the practice of being still and the answers will come if you're open and connected.

Chapter 3
Grateful Mind - Grateful Heart

"As we express our gratitude, we must never forget that the highest appreciation is not to utter words, but to live by them."
~ John F. Kennedy~

Gratitude does not just involve words; rather, it is a state of being. Gratitude originates with a thought and then flows to your heart and becomes a feeling. Once internalized, it becomes a way of living. As you learn to view all aspects of life through the lens of gratitude, your perceptions and attitudes will change. Obstacles become less debilitating and more productive. Gratitude is at the core of a positive mindset.

It's easy to be grateful for healthy relationships and positive people in your life. A grateful heart seems attainable when life is good. However, the challenge to maintain gratitude often comes during trials, poor health, loss, trauma, and the times when nothing seems to be going right.

Two months before my twenty-first birthday and six months before graduating college, my mother passed away. For four years, she suffered with a painful physical condition. At a pivotal age and time in my life, I watched my mother deteriorate physically, mentally, and emotionally. As previously discussed, she was my best friend and one of my closest confidants. We would have long, in-depth conversations, and when we couldn't talk, we would write letters. Overtime, she lost her ability to speak clearly, her short-term memory became foggy, and her fine motor skills and ability to write became difficult.

For some people, practicing gratitude in this circumstance may seem difficult or even impossible. How could I be grateful that at twenty-one years old, just when my adult life was beginning, my mother was gone? She wasn't by my side when I graduated college even though I took the fast track to attempt to graduate early due to her deteriorating condition. Although I graduated a semester early, it wasn't soon enough.

I'm not grateful for her death, her four years of suffering, or her absence from my life. My gratitude focuses on the life that she did live and the foundation she set for me. I'm grateful for the values she instilled, beliefs she held, and the lessons she taught me and my siblings. She was the core of our family, and the glue that held us together. Because of her, I learned the value and importance of unconditional love and support for family, especially in the difficult times. In her death, I learned to appreciate the preciousness of life, the value in sharing your feelings with those closest to you, and the significance of finding strength in yourself to survive.

My mom's death was at a key point of my life. At that time, I couldn't imagine finding gratefulness in losing her or turning her death into a positive experience. In fact, I ran from my grief and pain. It wasn't until later in life that I was able to find the gratitude. I miss her and feel sad at times when I think about my two sons missing out on meeting her and experiencing the love she had for all her children and grandchildren. Her life's purpose was being a wife, mother, and grandmother, and she lived it with great passion and strength.

One of the greatest gifts I received from her life and death is perseverance. I've learned to persevere through my pain, obstacles, and failures. It has been the key to overcoming and realizing life's glories. Once again, my deepest gratitude in this circumstance is in my mother's life and growing through her death.

How is gratitude achieved when you lose your job, which prevents you from paying your bills; when an illness prevents you from caring for yourself; or when a hurricane wipes out your home and all your belongings? I would be remiss in our current times to not address the impact of losing everything to a natural disaster. Tornados, earthquakes, hurricanes, fires, flooding and natural disasters of all kinds have occurred throughout the ages. However, they seem to be occurring more frequently. The devastation that is left in the path of some of these natural disasters is often incomprehensible. Yet people seem to overcome and are often able to rebuild. How do people recover from these devastating losses? It starts with a mindset shift, a determination to rebuild, and the decision to make the best of life despite adverse circumstances. Many times, those that survive a destructive natural disaster must focus on both survival and living life with gratitude.

When someone loses all their possessions, their life perspective shifts. Some people find it difficult to recover and may get caught up in their grief, anger, or fear and are unable to mentally recover. Those that choose to overcome, replace negative emotions with gratitude. Their energy and strength are focused on rebuilding and restoring their lives. Gratitude becomes their driving force. Their gratefulness is about their life and being alive.

One afternoon while I was out to lunch, I met a couple who lost their home and everything in it except for a photo album and some small mementos. They were taking some time away while waiting on the logistics of rebuilding their home in Florida. They shared their story of their incredible loss. It was obviously a painful experience, but after all this couple had lost, they disclosed their gratitude for each other and the miracle of their lives.

This traumatic event allowed the couple to gain a new perspective on life and shifted their priorities. The wife stated, "I never thought I'd speak these words, but I'm grateful we're able to start over. Losing the structure we called our home and all the belongings we accumulated has forced me to focus on the value of life and the love I have for my husband and family. Facetime with my granddaughter has become a daily occurrence." She shared that prior to this event, she took her husband for granted and was often critical of him. She had previously felt unhappy and dissatisfied. She is now living life with greater appreciation and a more positive perspective. Additionally, her marriage is stronger, and her critiques of her husband have greatly decreased.

Your circumstances may put you in a frame of mind that makes gratitude extremely difficult. Living in a constant state of gratitude takes practice and discipline. As with any mindset change, it takes a conscious effort. My youngest son played baseball from five years old. He was quite gifted with his athletic ability and played catcher and later, pitcher. His struggle was consistency with his hitting. We took him to a batting coach who worked with changing his batting stance. He'd kill it while with his batting coach but during game time, he'd revert back to the old stance. His coached explained that it would take 432 times for the new stance to become instinctive. After a lot of practice, his muscle memory kicked in, and the new stance became more natural. Similarly, a grateful mind is developed over time and takes energy to cultivate and sustain. It's a shift in perspective and needs to become a priority. A grateful mind breeds a grateful heart, which creates a life of hope.

Gratitude is not only significant in our grief or severe circumstances. Simple, daily gratitude is an essential part of changing your perspective. Open your eyes and be thankful for waking up, the flowers that brighten your yard, the sunshine, the rain that provides renewal, and the beauty of the creation around us. Some days it may be more difficult than others to embrace a grateful mind, but there is always something to be thankful for, even on the most difficult and stressful days.

A mindset of gratitude may take time to develop. Incorporating gratitude into to your daily routine, helps to integrate this type of thinking. Change takes time, so the more you practice, the quicker it becomes habitual. Each night, as you wrap up your day, develop a habit of writing in a gratitude journal. It can be as simple as making a list of five things you are grateful for from that day. Choose one of those items listed and expand upon on it or write a complete journal entry about something or someone you are grateful for from the day. Adding this exercise to your daily routine not only helps to create a more instinctively grateful mindset, but when done at bedtime, can lend to a more restful sleep. Research demonstrates that those with a grateful mind sleep better and are healthier overall.

Another strategy is to find ways to be grateful throughout the day. For myself, I begin each day with a prayer of gratitude and counting my blessings. In his podcast, Tony Robbins discussed that he "primes his mind" each morning by expressing his gratitude in prayer. Meditation is another way people can begin their day. Start your day with a gratitude meditation. In Jack Kornfield's book, "The Art of Forgiveness, Loving-kindness, and Peace," he discusses the practice of Buddhist monks beginning each day with a chant of gratitude for their blessings. He also shares that Native Americans began each ceremony with grateful prayers to mother earth and father sky. A grateful spirit is calmer, clearer, more energized, and joyful. The more you apply it throughout your day, the more natural it becomes, and the benefits become clearer and long-standing.

Expression of gratitude to others, benefits both that person and yourself. Don't be afraid or hold back on expressing your gratefulness. It's one thing to feel grateful and yet another to articulate it. Speaking gratitude makes it real and tangible. Sharing your appreciation for another builds them up and validates that person. Someone is more willing to go the extra mile when they feel appreciated. Throughout the years I've had numerous clients express their gratitude for something I said or a question I asked them. For me, this validates my purpose to help others grow and overcome their obstacles.

As a parent, there is nothing more rewarding than hearing your child express their gratitude for what you have contributed to his or her life. Or as a child, hearing a parent, teacher, coach or sibling tell you they are proud of you and recognize your effort and accomplishments. Think of the feeling when your spouse or partner shares their gratitude with you, especially when it's the daily things such as taking out the garbage or making dinner. Expressing and receiving thankfulness is not about ego, it's about support and validation. In general, most people are programmed to believe the negative comments and critiques. The rule of thumb is for every critique, one should offer two compliments. Expressing your appreciation for another is a tremendous compliment.

Creating a relationship with a foundation of gratitude makes it a much stronger and happier relationship. We should train our mind to focus on the positive in our relationships. There's a safety and trust that is built between people when there is an authentic appreciation for each other. Hearing a critique becomes more productive and less threatening. In all your relationships, make it habit to say thank you often. In general, a person will be more open and less defensive when a conversation begins with a positive statement or an expression of appreciation.

There is also a form of respect that comes from expressing gratitude. At a young age, my parents taught me to write thank you notes. I was taught that if someone took the time to think of you enough to show an act of kindness, then it is your responsibility to tell them thank you. How does it feel when you receive a note thanking you for a gift or some other act of kindness? On the contrary, how does it feel when you hold the door open for someone and they just walk past without as much as a nod of appreciation? Our intent for doing good deeds isn't for the "thank you," nor should it be. But when the action is validated, it creates a feeling of fulfillment.

We are created physiologically to give and receive gratitude. Our brain has what can be referred to as the reward system. The University of California Berkeley's, Greater Good Science Center, has conducted multiple studies which show that expressing thankfulness activates the reward system in the brain. These studies are specific to expressing and receiving gratitude from individuals. Additionally, a series of studies conducted by several medical professionals and published by "Oxford University Press," showed evidence that the hypothalamus is activated when we feel or express gratitude or conduct an act of kindness for another. The hypothalamus regulates hunger, sleep, body temperature and metabolism, which means that expressing and receiving thankfulness is good for our overall health.

When you share an expression of gratefulness, there's a feeling of happiness and satisfaction that follows. Similarly, being able to receive gratitude is just as important as expressing it to others. Allow others to show their appreciation for you, internalize it, and allow it to become integrated into your mind and heart.

Gratitude also impacts our emotions. Learning to be thankful in all circumstances can decrease anger and reactivity. Driving can often be a huge trigger for anger. The results of road rage can be costly, and in some cases, deadly. A mindset of gratitude while driving will change your initial reaction of anger to, "Thank God I just got my brake fixed! That could have been a bad wreck." Instead of, "What a jerk! I'll teach him to cut me off!" Our reactions to our children are different when we operate from a state of gratitude. For example, let's say that your daughter comes home late and doesn't call to let you know she'll be late. You're up worrying because this is not her typical behavior. She walks in and you say, "I'm so glad you're ok. Next time you're going to be late you need to call." Consequences are still important as a lesson for the behavior, but a calm conversation with a proactive solution would be more productive than one laced with anger. Becoming instinctively more grateful creates focus on first the positive and then the issue. It decreases reactivity and increases productivity

When someone deeply hurts us, violates us, or lets us down, finding gratitude may appear difficult. Our thankfulness is not in the act itself, it may be in the lesson we learned, strength we built, or action we took as a result of the behavior. Gratitude in all things includes relationships and people that have hurt us. We often learn and grow the most from these relationships, if we allow ourselves.

Learning to have gratefulness for all things makes life more beautiful and fulfilling. Take time to look at life through the lens of gratitude and see what happens internally.

Chapter 4
Embrace Your Obstacles

"Obstacles don't have to stop you.
If you run into a wall, don't turn around and give up. Figure
out how to climb it, go through it, or work around it"
~Michael Jordan~

It was the beginning of third grade when I first started being pulled out of class to go to Mrs. Gerrard's room. Mrs. G was my reading teacher and I'd go to her room three times a week. We would read books for about thirty minutes to help me overcome my reading comprehension disability. I could read without issue, but I couldn't recall what I had read. This obviously impacted my academics in grade school. Mrs. G was amazing, and to do this day, I am grateful for her because she wasn't only my reading teacher, but also was a support for me. Because I had to go to her room, my peers knew something was "wrong" with me. I remember being mocked, and it directly affected my self-confidence. It caused me to dislike school. I would get so stressed about going to school, and it would often make me physically ill.

Embrace Your Obstacles

During sixth grade, my parents pulled me out of the public school and sent me to the local Catholic school. Their hope was that it would be a chance for me to have a new start and make some new friends. The experience was positive. It took a while to adjust and feel as if I fit in with the others whom had all been going to school together since kindergarten. My socialization improved, but I still struggled academically. High school was slightly better, though it took me longer to complete tests and some assignments as compared to my peers. Although I was fearful of keeping up academically in college, I knew it was important for my future career.

I changed my major at the end of my freshman year due to the difficulty I was having in some classes. I was able to graduate with my business degree in three and half years, despite changing my major and still struggling academically. My drive was to graduate college while my mom was still alive. As I saw her condition dramatically declining each year, it propelled me to keep pushing through. I didn't allow my disability to prevent me from achieving this goal. Several years later, I was able to complete my master's program with straight A's! A huge accomplishment for me and now here I am writing a book.

Obstacles are something we all encounter. Without them, there wouldn't be a challenge to grow. Our biggest growth often comes from overcoming obstacles, traumas, and losses. An obstacle is merely a challenge to grow, learn and become stronger. You have a choice to either allow yourself to be overpowered by the stumbling blocks or overcome them. Everyone experiences roadblocks, but the key is how you choose to perceive them and the direction you choose to take when faced with them.

Have you ever wondered what life would be if you never had to experience trauma, loss, or disappointment? The reality is we all will encounter obstacles and traumas throughout our life, to varying degrees. Nothing happens by chance or coincidence, and we can't control our circumstances. However, when we realize each hurdle along our path has a purpose and can be an opportunity for our most significant change, we are provided the strength needed to leap over the hurdles.

It is our choice whether we give in and become victim to our obstacles or become the victor of our lives. Many years ago, my passion and purpose for choosing to become a counselor was to help people through trauma and grief. Many people have asked me how that can be my passion. The answer is because I've learned, through personal experience and observing others, that tremendous growth can result from pain. This has been reinforced through the numerous clients I've witnessed overcome some of the most severe circumstances one can endure.

One of the obstacles that I've dealt with for over twenty years is my struggle with Hashimoto, which is a thyroid disease that causes the thyroid gland to fluctuate. This can impact metabolism, focus, memory, emotions and other hormones in the body. There have been times when I've struggled with concentration, lack of motivation, lack of energy, weight fluctuations, anxiety and even apathy. After having this for over twenty years, I can quickly tell when my thyroid has fluctuated.

I have developed a healthy lifestyle and habits to help regulate my thyroid. As soon as I feel things are off, I've learned to take the necessary steps to get it regulated again. Due to the fluctuations, I need to make sure I don't get over-exhausted, exercise regularly, eat healthy and avoid certain foods which may trigger an imbalance.

There have been days that it's difficult to get out of bed and get motivated, but I know pushing myself is important. It would be easy to give in to the symptoms and allow them to take control, but I've chosen to take charge and not allow them to interfere with my daily functioning. Taking care of myself is not an option, it's a must.

Being attune to your body and emotions is also key to keeping things in check. Knowing when it's time to reach out to health professionals, increase rest, or other self-care options becomes a priority. As a coach and counselor, it is important that I'm focused and fully present for my clients. Therefore, rather than giving in to the symptoms and allowing them to prevent me from functioning at my best for my clients, I've determined that I will not allow this disease to prevent me from achieving my goals and living my life. I will not give in and use this as an excuse to not live fully.

Personally, I know many people who struggle with health issues of varying degrees. It's not always easy to push through the effects of every illness, and some may not be able to control all the symptoms or side effects. However, when it comes to physical illnesses, you can control your mindset and how you view your symptoms. There is plenty of research that shows how mind over matter can impact disease. The perspective you take when receiving a diagnosis can have a direct impact on the progression and how you choose to live with your diagnosis. Even when diagnosed with a terminal illness such as a stage 4 cancer, you can have an impact on your prognosis with a positive mindset.

With the rising rate of cancer diagnoses, the majority of us know or have known someone with cancer. Personally, I've known several people whose perspective and state of mind affected their diagnosis. One particular person stands out in my mind. Jennifer was fifty-years-old and diagnosed with a severe case of bone cancer. This woman was the glue that held her family together. She was the caretaker for several family members and a person who never stood idle. As many who receive the diagnosis of stage 4 cancer, or any cancer, she initially was in shock.

She experienced the various emotions that go along with such a diagnosis such as anxiety, sadness, and anger. She chose to remain positive and hopeful and faced each day with gratitude and perseverance. Her prognosis was six months, and she made a list of things she wanted to do in that time frame. She created a timeline and began checking everything off her list. There wasn't anything that held her back. She rested when necessary and followed all the protocols.

Ultimately the cancer took her life, but she exceeded the 6 month prognosis to a year. She could have given in to the cancer and allowed herself to be angry, fearful, or depressed. No one would have blamed her. Instead, she chose to live her life and accomplish everything on her list. Through her determination and perseverance, she chose to continue to live and overcame her fear and pain.

During one of our conversations, she told me that although she didn't understand why she had cancer, she embraced her faith and accepted that this was part of God's plan. She wanted to show her family and her children, that no matter what life hands you, it's always possible to be positive and make the best of all circumstances. Her physicians were amazed at her ability to push through her pain. Bone cancer can be one of the most painful types of cancer one can experience. Jennifer didn't stop until the very last week of her life, and the doctors were certain it was her determination and mindset that kept her going.

Her children remember their mom as a strong, positive, and faithful woman. Of course, they miss her and feel sadness, but they are confident that their mother gave it all she could and admire her for remaining positive and living her life to the fullest. To endure the pain with determination to accomplish her checklist of adventures without complaint or hesitation, taught them the power of their own minds to overcome obstacles.

During one of my trips to the beach, I met a man named Denny who had his leg amputated due to diabetes. At the time we met, I had just finished a run on the beach. I was walking up the stairs that led to the hotel, and he was sitting on the steps drinking his coffee. He asked me how my run was and how many miles I had run. He told me about how he used to enjoy jogging on the beach. Seeing that he had a prosthetic leg, I asked how long it had been since he had jogged. He said that he had only had his prosthetic for about two months, but it had been a couple years since he had run.

He explained that when he was young, he didn't take care of himself. Despite his diabetes, he had been a heavy drinker until about four years ago. His doctor had told him he needed to start taking care of his body as he began having more health issues. He started jogging and would visit his parents who were retired and lived near the beach in Panama City, Florida. He really enjoyed jogging on that beach, but unfortunately, his years of poor health maintenance caught up with him, and his leg had to be amputated.

One of his goals was to begin jogging again. As we talked, it became clear that not only had Denny made changes with his health and exercise, he had also learned he needed to change his thinking. He had a positive outlook on his future and knew he had to forgive himself for abusing his body for so many years. Denny admitted he had gone into a depression for a brief time prior to the surgery, but his doctor sent him to a therapist who helped him refocus. He told me he wanted to speak to adolescents who have been diagnosed with diabetes and hoped through sharing his story, he could help them realize the importance of taking care of themselves.

He also shared that while in therapy, he realized he was angry that he had diabetes. His drinking had become a false sense of control. He has since learned that he could have control over his disease, and instead of letting it beat him down and destroy his body more, he has chosen to keep healthy habits and use his experience to try to help others. Once again, another story of someone who could have easily chosen to give in to his illness and let it have control. He created a purpose out of his amputation instead of allowing it to become a roadblock.

Illness, disease, or other physical ailments aren't the only obstacles we may face. There are numerous things that can get in our way of living. Financial hardships, failed relationships, loss of loved ones, job loss, natural disasters and other various tragedies. The key is in your choice. You choose how much an obstacle will prevent you from living the life you have been created to live. An obstacle is merely an opportunity for growth. Without them, what would motivate change? The way you persevere through tragedy, loss, and challenge creates character.

My two sons grew up in motorsports, and they both shared with me how it taught them a lot about life and overcoming disappointment, obstacles, and perseverance. The racetrack can be an analogy for life. The drivers, families, friends, and crews spend numerous hours

Embrace Your Obstacles

preparing for a race. Many drivers and families make financial sacrifices to afford to be able to race. And in a split second, any number of events can occur to end your day at the racetrack. A driver can lead the entire race, and in the final lap, the engines blows. Two cars can crash into each other and the cars are destroyed. A tire blows, car runs out of fuel, a part on the car breaks, or other challenges occur. Yet the drivers, teams, families and friends show up the next week to do it all over again.

The reward of winning the race or series championship, setting a track record, and ultimately living out a dream keeps them going. Racing can present many volatile circumstances. One moment, you can be in the lead, and in a matter seconds, you're last. A driver may have the best season of their life and a sponsor pulls out, leaving the driver without a ride. Or you can be the most talented driver, but without the financial backing, you aren't given an opportunity. Despite these conditions, there's a drive and motivation to keep pursuing the dream of winning or making it into the highest level of the drivers chosen path. The adrenaline and excitement when one arrives at the racetrack is worth all the disappointment and obstacles.

We all face obstacles, unexpected events occur, promises are broken, and at any given moment, something tragic can happen. But it's important to push through and follow our path, passion and vision. Allowing obstacles, challenges, and losses to prevent us from moving forward or blocking our dreams, prevents us from potential growth. It's in the glory of overcoming an obstacle that brings us authentic happiness and peace.

The perspective you have and maintain in all circumstances will determine your success at persevering through life's roadblocks. Believing that nothing is by chance or coincidence will carry you through any obstacle. Everyone we meet along our journey is present for a reason, season, or lifetime. Some relationships are to teach a lesson, and some are to validate our path and provide support. Others are to join us on our journey for a lifetime. Trusting in yourself may take time, but once you fully trust in your abilities and strength, you can tackle any challenge that comes your way.

In October 2016 my sweet nephew passed away. He was only 22-years-old just shy of his twenty-third birthday. His death was unexpected, and I can only imagine the pain my brother and sister-in-law felt at that time and still feel. Yet their strength has been inspirational. They both have strong faith, and it's my belief, that is what sustained them and allowed them to persevere. For me, losing my nephew was difficult, but I believe he is in Heaven looking down upon us all with his amazing huge smile. Attending his funeral was surreal but seeing how many people attended, listening to his friends telling stories, and later seeing the comments his friends continue to leave on his Facebook page, help me to realize the lives he touched. They all seem to comment on his smile and his ability to cheer others up. It is touching to see the positive impact he had on his friends' lives.

Making sense of the loss of such a young life is difficult, and yet believing that he lived out his purpose and is now in a place of peace and joy is comforting. It's all a part of a bigger plan and knowing that my brother and sister-in-law have the same faith is comforting. Life is meant to be lived and we truly honor our deceased loved ones best when we choose to make the most out of our lives here on earth.

Sometimes it takes looking at another person's struggles or story to move past our own obstacles. As a counselor for almost twenty years, I've heard some of the saddest and most horrific stories, yet I'm also privileged to have witnessed some of these people overcome their tragedies. The stories of severe abuse, neglect, rejection, and trauma can be overwhelming, but I remain encouraged by the tremendous growth and confidence that can come out of these stories. To watch people go from feeling defeated, small, beaten down, and raw to glowing, confident, and passionate is simply amazing.

The Mindset Makeover

The story of Dave Pelzer and his first book, "A Child Called It," were a huge inspiration for me in deciding to get my master's in counseling. It's a true story of a young boy, Dave, who grew up in California and was tortured and severely abused by his mother. He was able to survive because of his faith and his positive mindset. There are additional books by Dave that tell his story as he grows up and becomes a man. But the point of surviving such torture from a young developmental age, is a true testament to how determination, faith, and a positive mindset can pull you through anything.

There are an abundance of stories of survival and how people have overcome adversity, abuse, poverty, and numerous other traumas and tragedies. There have been cases of positive significant change that come from people who have survived and turned tragedy into triumph. As previously stated, life's obstacles build our character and are part of who we become. The next time you are faced with an obstacle, choose to look at it as a challenge to conquer and an opportunity to build your character.

Instead of allowing an unforeseen circumstance to become a roadblock or reason to quit, choose to find a way to push through it. Try something new and challenge yourself to be strong rather than give up. If the obstacle you face is rejection, or failure, keep going and don't give up. A quote by C.S. Lewis sums it up. He said, "Hardships often prepare ordinary people for an extraordinary destiny."

It's not about the obstacle, loss, rejection or failure; it's about how you push through that defines your character. So many times I've seen the tremendous glory that is on the other side of the struggle. Your trials are not a predictor of who you are or will become. Your mind and faith are your greatest assets when faced with any obstacle. The internal message you tell yourself is the key to survival and success. There is no obstacle so great that you can't overcome it. Believe it with all your mind, heart and soul. As you overcome your obstacles, you learn to love more, take more chances, and discover an inner strength that propels you to live a fulfilled life.

Chapter 5

Fearful to Fearless

"Fear kills growth. "
~ Gary Vaynerchuk ~

Fear is the number one killer of dreams. When we give in to the power of fear, we surrender the life we were created to live. Fear keeps us stagnate and prevents us from growing. It comes from a sense that you are in danger or potentially facing either emotional or physical trauma. The fear of the unknown, fear of failure, fear of what others think, and fear of death. The reality is, fear is all in your mind. Learning that you are the operator of your mind and in control of your thoughts is also recognizing that you have control over your fears.

One area of my expertise as a counselor is treating people who struggle with Obsessive, Compulsive Disorder (OCD). One form of treatment is called Exposure Response Prevention (ERP). To briefly explain, this is a treatment where the client is exposed to situations, objects, images, or thoughts that trigger anxiety and/or the obsession. Once the anxiety has been triggered, the response prevention part of the treatment is resisting the urge for the compulsive behavior. Ultimately, the goal of this treatment is reducing or eliminating the obsessive thinking, anxiety, and compulsive behavior. Allowing the client to live a more peaceful and satisfying life. According to the, International OCD Foundation, this treatment, has been found to be one of the most effective therapeutic forms of treating OCD. Face the fear to overcome it.

Similarly, exposure therapy is a treatment used to help people suffering from anxiety. It's a similar concept of exposing the person to that which triggers the anxiety. Often times, anxiety leads to avoidance and can prevent someone from experiencing all the joys of life that others may take for granted. Anxiety is similar to fear and taking charge of that anxiety is equivalent to taking charge of fear. As a therapist, I've treated numerous clients utilizing these methods, and I've seen them work. I've witnessed firsthand the joy, gratitude and pure exhilaration these clients experience when they've completed their treatment. When they realize they have the power to conquer their fears, anxiety, and compulsions, they experience life with peace and joy.

Triumphs include the man who can provide for his family because he no longer fears exposure to germs. The young girl who can go to her friend's sleepover and stay through the night without debilitating fear that something will happen to her mom while she's away. The woman who can fulfill her lifelong dream of visiting the country where her ancestors came from because she has overcome her fear of heights and flying. The list goes on and on.

The effectiveness of these treatments has been proven by various professional organizations, scientific research, universities and healthcare professionals. In my opinion, they are effective because they help the client experience the very thing that triggers their fear, anxiety, and need for compulsive behaviors. The exposure treatments allow people to face and then conquer their fears. The best cure of fear is to face, touch, see, and feel the very obstacle that has prevented them from living a purposeful life.

We all have the ability to conquer our fears. We have the power within to take charge and not let fear hold us back. After my divorce I was filled with several fears. How was I going to make it on my own? How would I survive the loneliness? What are people going to think? Will I lose friends? Will my boys be angry with me? What about my spiritual life? Will I lose clients? And on and on. Unfortunately, with the skyrocketing rate of divorce, I'm sure many of you can relate to some of these fears and thoughts.

Overtime I began to tackle my fears and work through them. Today, I am a lot stronger and less fearful because of conquering those fears. I'm more willing to take chances and push myself beyond my limits. I'm genuinely, authentically enjoying life. Do I still have fears or experience a bit of anxiety? Absolutely! But I've learned to tackle them and not allow them to hold me back.

The fear of failure and rejection are two fears that hinder so many people. They say things like: What if I don't succeed? What if the whole thing falls apart? What if I lose everything? What if people think I'm crazy? Stop "what-ifing" and start doing. We can all get caught up in the "what-ifs" of life. When our "what-ifs" are based in fear and negativity, we stop really living. When those "what-ifs" transform into faith filled, positive statements, they can look something like this: "What if" you are successful? "What if" life is better than you've ever imagined? "What if" you could feel more fulfilled?

A fearless mindset answers the, "What if I fail?" question with, "Then I'll try again." Or "I'll learn from the experience and continue trying." The most successful people have failed numerous times. Colonel Sanders, founder of Kentucky Fried Chicken was turned down over a 1000 times before he found someone to accept his secret recipe and idea to begin a franchise. By the way, he was sixty-two when the first franchise opened. He didn't let fear of rejection or failure get in his way.

Michael Jordan didn't make the varsity high school team his first time trying out. He didn't let that stop him and became arguably one of the greatest basketball players of all time. It has been documented in various reports that it took Thomas Edison over 10,000 attempts to invent the light bulb. According to an article by "Business Insider," Harrison Ford was told after his first small movie role that he would not be successful in the movie business. Sir James Dyson had over 5,000 failed prototypes before he came up with the one vacuum that is now the bestselling bagless vacuum on the market.

At a Tony Robbins event in Atlanta, Georgia, he discussed that he had failed at a million things while working at achieving his goals. Yet, he never gave up and because of his perseverance, has not only gained tremendous success but has also helped millions of people improve their lives. The list can go on, but clearly some of the most successful and inspirational people have failed and been rejected numerous times.

If fear is in control, you'll miss out on realizing your full potential. When you focus on your fear, you allow it to take hold. Tony Robbins says, "Where focus goes, energy flows." He uses this quote in reference to focusing on your dreams, goals, and achieving success. However, it applies to anything you focus on. When you focus on fear, your energy is going there too. Your energy needs to be on your purpose and attaining your goals and dreams.

Conquering fear gives way to determination and drive. Instead of giving energy to fear, direct it towards overcoming fear. Look it in the face and say, "I'm not letting you win! I will prove you wrong!" Allow fear to create positive momentum to direct your path in a productive way. Release fear from its hold on your life. If it is preventing you from living out your purpose or embracing your passion, then it's time to release it from your mind.

Fear, worry, and anxiety are often culprits of sleep deprivation. How many sleepless nights have you had because of the power of fear or worry? Worrying has never changed the outcome or prevented something from happening. Anxiety interferes with productivity.

Early on in my career as a therapist, I primarily worked with children and adolescents. One of my favorite exercises to do with them was creating a worry box. The purpose of the box is to hold the worry, fear, or anxiety, which allows the client to free it from his or her mind. Before going to bed, the client writes down any fears or worries and places them in the box. Then he or she focuses on the five things they are grateful for. The majority of the time, my clients received a more restful sleep. Similarly, some of my clients use visualization to accomplish the same goal.

In Joe Gibbs' book, "Game Plan for Life," he discusses how all anxiety does is keep you from rest. His solution is to hand it over to God. The Bible says, "Do not be anxious about anything, but in every situation, by prayer and petition, with thanksgiving, present your requests to God." (Philippians 4:6). Remember, anxiety is our fears.

As a coach and NASCAR owner, Joe has helped many athletes overcome fear and direct their focus on the end game. Whether it's winning a game, winning a race, or winning at life, focus needs to be on the forward direction of your purpose. Finding a way to let go of the fear creates more rest, which allows you to have more energy for a positive focus.

Sometimes fear comes from past experiences. If you were in a relationship that ended in a broken heart, fear may keep you from allowing yourself to feel vulnerable again. The fear of feeling that deep pain again may prevent you from discovering a truly loving and lasting relationship. The reality is you may get hurt again, but you may find the most amazing love you have ever known.

Let's slow down for a moment. Put the book down and think of one of your fears. Imagine how you'd feel if you faced that fear and won. Imagine the feelings and thoughts you would experience. There is nothing more invigorating than the feeling you get after you've conquered a fear.

Several years ago, I attended a hot air balloon festival with some friends. We had all decided to take a ride in one of the balloons. Kelly not only had a fear of heights, but also a fear of flying. After several minutes of talking and helping her breath and relax, she agreed to join us. As we began to take off, I could see the fear in her pale expression. She gripped my hand so tightly I thought she would cut off my circulation. Once she allowed herself to relax, she released my hand and began to enjoy the beauty below us. Her fear turned to excitement and by the time we landed, Kelly was like a child on Christmas morning. She was giddy with laughter. She was so excited that she had tackled her fears and didn't allow them to prevent her from enjoyment. There was a new confidence about Kelly after that moment. She learned that she can convince herself to push fear aside just as easily as she had been convincing herself to stay in her fear.

If fear is preventing you from following your dreams, ask yourself why you're allowing it? Is the debilitating fear more valuable than the joy, peace, and fulfillment you will feel when you achieve your goals? Focus on all the good you can do, the enjoyment you'll have, and the growth you'll experience as you live life with purpose and intent.

Getting out of bed will be easier, the sun will appear brighter, relationships will be richer, and life will be more meaningful.

Don't let fear hinder you, instead let it be a driving force. You have control over your fear. Fear feeds doubt and stagnation and prevents forward movement. Our mind will believe what we allow it to believe. Don't allow fear to prevent you from living and experiencing life. Remember, on the other side of fear is freedom!

Chapter 6

Forgiveness

"Forgiveness does not change the past, but it does enlarge the future. "
~Paul Boese~

Forgiveness is often the most difficult concept for people to embrace and yet a skill we all must master. There is so much ugliness in this world today. It's senseless to hold grudges especially over trivial things. You need stay focused on what is really important. Take circumstances where others have hurt you or offended you and use them as motivation to make a difference.

Equally as productive is taking ownership of what you have done wrong and forgiving yourself. Whenever I approach the topic of forgiveness with my clients, it evokes a "deer in the headlights" response. It is a difficult task to undertake. Furthermore, the forgiveness of self is even more difficult. The act of forgiveness is not to say the behavior that created the hurt is acceptable. It's about letting go of the hurt or pain that was caused.

Healing from others' transgressions against you can't be complete without forgiveness. The task of forgiveness is more attainable when we embrace the concept that none of us are perfect or without fault. No matter our intent, it is a guarantee that we will let someone down. We cannot please everyone all the time. In fact, we will even let ourselves down now and then. Therefore, it is inevitable that we all need to give and receive forgiveness.

We cannot control how another person responds to our apology nor can we expect others to ask us for forgiveness. The way someone else accepts or rejects our apology is a reflection on where that person is in their life. The benefit of a genuine apology is more for the one offering it than the one receiving it. Asking for forgiveness helps to move past regret, pain, or guilt. Our character is built when we take responsibility for our actions and realize the that we may have negatively impacted someone else.

An apology should be genuine and authentic for it to be meaningful. If you are truly sorry for your actions, words, or choices, then apologize. As long as you are respectful and empathetic to others you should never have to apologize for your beliefs or values.

Forgiveness frees you from others' actions or words and not allowing them to control your thoughts and feelings. Once I came to terms with forgiving my ex-husband for not being the partner I needed, for not loving me the way I needed to be loved, for all the false accusations and hurtful words, and not hearing the truth, I felt free and no longer burdened by my past. I felt empowered and discovered that I am good enough, strong enough and capable enough to find peace and security within myself. I don't need to believe the lies of the past or live with the old internal story that had developed.

I realized that my ex-husband's actions and words were his own pain and need for healing from his past. He was unable to feel the love I was giving, and I couldn't provide love he needed. Even though I tried my best, it wasn't enough for his inner peace and happiness. And what he had to give wasn't enough for my sustained psychological and physical health. Once again, we cannot be all things to everyone at all times. Recognizing the unhealthy patterns and failed attempts at change, was the point of realizing it was time to move forward. Holding any hurt, anger, resentment or grudges was only hurting myself.

This was also a process of forgiving myself. No one walks down the aisle hoping to someday go through divorce. Once I came to terms with forgiving him, I was then able to forgive myself and let go of false thinking that I was a failure. I had to forgive myself for not being enough for my ex-husband, for feeling as if I failed as a mother, and for letting my sons down. I had to let go of the guilt that I had let my family down, though I logically knew that wasn't the case because they had been my biggest support.

As the youngest of six, I am the first and only one to experience divorce. This added to my guilt, but I was able to forgive myself and realize I did the best I could within my ability to make things work. Sometimes there comes the point that you realize there is no resolution and closing the chapter is the best option.

As for my sons, I apologized to them, and they have both assured me they forgive me. Though I'm sure they would rather have their parents together, they want us both to be happy and live our dreams. They are both incredible young men. They are living life with purpose and passion and striving to realize their visions. They realize that sometimes two people are healthier apart and know they are loved. Our divorce didn't impact my unconditional love for them.

On November 21, 2002, at approximately 6:00 am, my then husband and myself were awakened by our phone ringing. I instantly knew in my gut that this wasn't going to be good news. It was my sister calling to tell us that my dad had been in an accident and was in serious condition at the hospital. As my ex-husband was talking to my sister, I felt

Forgiveness

overwhelmed with emotion and knew my dad wasn't in "serious condition." He was gone.

At the time, my ex-husband, myself, and our two sons were living in California, and my father lived in the suburbs of Chicago. He was coming to visit us for Thanksgiving. He lived within a few blocks of a Holiday Inn, and they would allow him to use their airport shuttle when he traveled. As he was walking in a crosswalk across a four-lane road, he was hit and killed by a car. It was shock, panic, sadness, and anger all at once!

My first question was, "Did the driver stop?" And yes, he had stopped. He had not only stopped, but per witnesses, he put his coat over my father, held him and was seen crying. We will never truly know what happened or why this man wasn't able to avoid hitting him. I can't even imagine what thoughts were in his head after the accident. Once my shock wore off, I knew in my heart I needed to forgive this man. But how do you forgive the person who took the life of your father? My father had become my best friend and the man who my two boys looked up to and loved with all their hearts. My dad was so proud of my two sons. He was an integral part of their early childhood. He was their biggest fan and cheerleader. He enjoyed watching them race their Quarter Midgets and play baseball. He created lasting memories for them. Whenever he visited, he would take them on long walks and created a tradition of taking them out to breakfast.

When we moved to California and purchased our first home, he came and met all our neighbors long before we had met them. My father was a great example of what a loving and devoted husband looks like and an equally loving father and wonderful grandfather. His priority was his family, and he enjoyed visiting his children, grandchildren, and siblings.

Forgiveness is easier when you have the mindset that everything happens for a reason. Nothing is by chance. There are no coincidences. Every person we meet and circumstance we encounter is part of our life's journey. It's up to us to decide how we respond. A couple nights before my father's accident, I had a dream. I woke from my dream with tears running down my face. In my dream, my deceased mother was sitting on the end of my bed and rubbing my leg. She was telling me, "It will all be alright." She was always the one to comfort me when I was young. This dream obviously disturbed me, but I didn't know what it meant. Fast forward to a couple hours before we received the phone call about my dad, and I woke with a feeling in my gut. It was that uneasy feeling we sometimes get. I had an urge to call my dad but convinced myself that was silly. It was 2:00 am and he was supposed to be coming later that day.

After receiving the call, I had a flash of just about every emotion one can have in that moment. There was an urgency to go to him. I went upstairs to grab a duffle bag from my then ten-year-old son's room. As I entered his room, he sat up in bed and said, "Papa was here." My heart sunk as I knew I needed to tell him the news. "Mom he was here. He was standing right there." As he said this, he pointed to the entryway to his computer nook. "He was smiling. He had his cane in his hand and was dressed in his long black coat…" He proceeded to describe exactly what my father was wearing. We didn't know until later, when the hospital gave us his belongings, that my father was wearing the exact clothing my son had described.

Putting all these pieces together was evidence that it was part of a plan. Many questions flooded my mind. Why did this have to happen? What were we all to learn from this? For each of us who loved him, the answers are different. And we may never get the answers we were looking for. All I knew was that my heart needed to forgive. As tragic as this is, holding onto any anger or bitterness wouldn't bring my father back. It wouldn't reverse that day. This man has to live with this the rest of his life with this accident on his conscious. My hope is that he was able to do something positive from this experience.

Much later, my siblings and I saw this man. I saw remorse in his eyes, which helped with the process of forgiveness. My dad was an overall a healthy man. He was independent, helped so many people, and truly loved his family. One of his biggest fears he had was having to depend on other people. He feared the day he would lose his driver's license due to age. Well, he never had to experience any of this and was able to live in the home I was raised in. He was able to travel and visit his children, grandchildren, and siblings. He attended church every morning when he wasn't traveling. His church dedicated "his" seat in his name.

My father lived a full life and was loved by so many. He was admired by my boys and brought so much laughter and good memories to their lives. I find gratitude in the fact that he didn't have to suffer from health issues or ever become dependent on others as I know that would have brought him shame. And I'm positive his last thoughts were good ones.

Forgiveness comes when we can let go. When we can find a lesson in the pain or realize that nothing is by chance and there is a purpose for every event in our life. We all have a purpose, but we never know when our time is done.

Forgiveness cleanses our soul and frees our thoughts and feelings for more positive outlooks. It's letting go of the past so we can clearly see our future. Holding on to anger, bitterness, and pain gives another person control over your life. Forgiving them releases their control and allows you freedom to move forward.

Kelly was a one of my first clients after obtaining my counseling license. She had grown up in a household that was full of anger and fear. She had been severely abused physically and mentally by her mother and step-father. Kelly's biological father died when she was three years old. Her mother met her step-father and married him within a year of her father's death. She was never allowed to talk about her father or grieve his death. The abuse she experienced was truly inconceivable, and she felt her survival was a miracle. She also witnessed her mother being hit by her step-father. Being an only child, she didn't have anyone growing up to confide in. Throughout her childhood, she felt alone and fearful.

Kelly came to me when she was in her late twenties and pregnant with her first child. She had been in and out of counseling for a few years and understood she was a survivor. She had worked through much of the trauma and frightening memories. She learned how to cope with anxiety and overcome her fears. More importantly, she separated herself from her parents as she realized it was a toxic relationship. Kelly had met a kind and loving young man while in college, and they married right after graduation. She felt her life was heading in the right direction and was excited about being a mom.

Kelly's concern was the lingering anger inside, which felt like rage at times. She identified various triggers and realized that she was holding onto resentments and anger from the past. Kelly wanted to release this intense anger, so she could be healthy both emotionally and physically once her baby arrived. She needed to forgive her step-father and mother in order to free herself of the pent-up anger, hurt, and resentment. It took a few sessions, but ultimately, she was able to forgive and let go. Her forgiveness came upon realizing that forgiving them didn't excuse their unacceptable behavior. She was able to realize her own strength and strong values that she had developed on her own from this experience.

Kelly chose to not remain under their control any longer. She realized that all she had been through made her the woman she was today. She developed a strong value system and aligned her perspective with the vision she had for her life as a wife and mother. Despite the lack of a healthy example, she knew the type of home and family she wanted. Kelly had the strength and determination to break the cycle and overcome her own fears.

She was able to forgive because she believed they were so damaged themselves they didn't know better. In the process, she also realized the suppressed anger she felt for her biological father. She was angry that he had died and abandoned her. She hadn't realized until she forgave her mother, that she blamed him for all of it. Kelly was able to forgive all her parents, and as she described it, felt as free as an eagle soaring through the sky.

Holding onto the anger keeps you stuck in the past. It's like dragging an anchor around throughout your life. It prevents you from fully moving forward. Sometimes people project their unresolved anger onto others and cause pain. It becomes a cycle that can continue if we don't find a way to forgive and let go. Realizing that everyone who has caused pain in your life made you stronger and helped you develop your character, eases the process of forgiveness. We can't control how others will choose to treat us, but we can control how we respond.

A bully is looking to inflict his or her own pain onto another. An abuser is looking to have control or dominance, and like a bully, there's a strong likelihood that he or she was abused or neglected. In either case, the behavior is not acceptable, but your forgiveness actually removes their power. You take away their control over you. Forgiving those who have hurt you releases their stronghold on your life and your future.

Forgiveness should be a consistent practice. It's not just needed for the big things, but for the seemingly small things as well. Forgiveness is also for the friend who cancelled your lunch date for the third time, the guy who just cut you off on the highway, or your husband for not emptying the dishwasher. In fact, learning to forgive the small stuff makes it less difficult to forgive the big stuff.

As you learn to forgive the daily transgressions of others, you build an empathetic mindset. You become more patient and less stressed. When we hold on to the smaller irritations, it's like a volcano building pressure until it eventually erupts. A better strategy is to allow a frequent and gradual release of hurt and anger through forgiveness. Furthermore, learning to forgive all things builds healthy, happy and lasting relationships.

The hardest person to forgive is usually ourselves. We are often harder on ourselves than we are on others. We must wholeheartedly forgive ourselves for our mistakes, misfortunes, poor choices, and hurting others. All the guilt, regret, and self-sabotage is heavy to carry. Writing is a healthy way to heal and release emotions. Write a letter of forgiveness to yourself - for your past, present and even future mistakes. Being human means, we are imperfect. It's guaranteed you will make mistakes, you will hurt or let others down, and you will make a poor choice. Remember, it is often in those moments that we grow the most. When you realize you messed up, rather than beating yourself up, look at the situation and reflect on how you could have done it differently. Reflect on why you made the choice. Were you reactive? Were you fearful? Were your intentions pure? And then forgive yourself.

Holding onto guilt, regret or anger prevents you from growth. The weight of carrying around all your emotional baggage can get so heavy and cause mental exhaustion, which leads to depression. Forgiveness is one of the best gifts you can give yourself. It's telling yourself you are human and make mistakes. You must understand that you are not perfect and acknowledge the error of your ways. You are just as worthy of forgiveness as those you have forgiven.

As you learn to forgive yourself, you also gain more awareness of how your actions and words impact others. Being more conscious of your responses towards others develops an empathetic mindset and a character of integrity. Learning to be less reactive and increasing self-control lessens the need to forgive.

Forgiveness is purging your mind of negative thoughts. It's not forgetting or accepting poor behavior. It just removes judgement. The Bible teaches us not to judge or we will be judged and to forgive if we want forgiveness. We must learn from our mistakes and the mistakes of others. Sometimes, the hurt others cause, teaches us who we don't want to be. It can motivate us to do better and develop a greater moral compass.

There is no purpose to be served by spending our energy focused on the past and what pain others have caused us or we have caused. It's important that we live and learn, and once we've learned, we don't go back and repeat the same mistakes over. The important take away is that we do forgive others as well as ourselves. Forgiveness isn't about the act but rather about letting go so you can move forward with a clearer mindset.

Chapter 7
Relationships

"There will always be people in your life who treat you wrong. Be sure to thank them for making you strong."
~Zig Ziglar~

The influence of those you spend the most time with has significance on your thoughts and mindset. Healthy relationships are those that support your goals and dreams, and those which share the same values. They are validating and encouraging. A healthy relationship enhances our life and helps build trust. Life is richer, when we are surrounded by people who accept us and walk beside us on our journey.

On the other hand, toxic relationships are draining and distracting. They add doubt and discouragement to our lives. Toxic relationships are a hindrance to achieving fulfillment and developing a positive mindset. Surrounding yourself with others who have differing views or goals can enhance your life. We don't all share the same perspectives; however, be cautious when spending time with people who choose negativity or drain your emotions.

Setting healthy boundaries with others helps keep your mind positively focused on your life's purpose and goals. Constant negative influences are a distraction. The key is to surround yourself with those who support, motivate, and validate you. You don't have to share the same goals to be supportive.

We can have differing views and still maintain a positive relationship when there is mutual respect. It's easier to have a healthy relationship when we know what to expect. Sometimes it's necessary to lower our expectations of people in our lives. If you have someone up on a pedestal, the only direction they can go is down. Remember, people will let us down. We are not perfect, and relationships take effort. Whether it's a family member, friend or significant other, they all take work and at the core of all relationships is trust and honesty. The only control we have in our relationships is how we act and express ourselves. We cannot control the other person or expect them to know our needs if we don't share them. Setting boundaries for what is acceptable and unacceptable is healthy.

Being confident and knowing your own limits and needs, sets a solid foundation for all your relationships. Furthermore, how you allow others to treat you is an indicator of the health of your inner psyche. A difference in a healthy relationship and an unhealthy one is how you

Relationships

each handle the adversity in the relationship. The key to any relationship is communication and trust. Being clear through words and actions allows others to know your expectations and needs. It's easier to trust someone when they are open and consistent with their words and actions.

If someone has let you down, don't keep it in and let it fester. Tell them what they have done or said and how it has affected you. Be respectful with your words and how you express your emotions. Blaming, shaming, or accusing will lead to defensiveness and not be productive. Rather than blaming the other person, state how you feel, and if appropriate, why it is you feel that way. Expressing our feelings is a good release. Once you have expressed yourself, allow there to be a discussion and hear each other out. Allowing things to build up is not productive and often leads to further hurt and resentments, which aren't healthy in any relationship. Keeping our mind clear of negativity breeds a healthier relationship.

It's not healthy or fair to others if we don't verbalize how we feel. Rather than gossiping, go directly to the source. Give the other person a chance to clarify their intentions or realize how their actions or words have impacted you. Often, people are unaware of how they affect others. You may be the only person who is honest and perhaps may be the catalyst for positive change. If you are agitated with someone, it's your responsibility to communicate your feelings. Once you've expressed yourself, it is then on the other person to decide how they will process and react to you.

When a relationship becomes toxic, there may be no other choice but to completely sever the ties. Negative-minded people drain you of your energy and motivation. Overtime you may begin to internalize the negative criticism and doubt yourself. Toxic relationships distract you from your goals and have you question your values and beliefs. If someone has you doubting yourself, try to have a conversation. If there isn't any change, then it may be time to distance yourself from that person. It's not necessary to create a volatile exit, just respectfully walk away.

Sometimes walking away isn't easy. If it's a family member, you may just need to minimize your interactions. Mentally prepare yourself before seeing this person, telling yourself you will not allow their negative energy into your mind. If the environment becomes too heavy, you will walk away. Taking care of yourself daily is crucial to cope with others who choose negativity. The more confident you are within yourself, the easier it is to deflect those whom counter what you believe. Nurturing your internal voice builds a strong mindset. Feeding yourself positive thoughts and words is a healthy way to build your own inner strength and confidence.

Keeping your inner circle small minimizes the likelihood for distractions and unnecessary stress. Remember, it's not about the quantity but the quality of the relationships you have in your life. Your inner circle is those whom you spend the most time with, confide in and seek advice or guidance from. They should be the ones who share in your joy and accomplishments, support you when you fail, and motivate you to keep going. Your inner circle is also those that will have the most influence on your mindset. The more time you spend with someone the more you internalize their words and develop similar habits.

That is why it's important to choose those who share similar values, will be honest with you, enhance your life, and validate your visions. They should not be judgmental or discourage your dreams or goals. Your inner circle should be relationships that are reciprocal, balanced and healthy.

Beyond your inner circle are those friends, acquaintances, colleagues and perhaps family members who are in your life that you care about. These are the people who you may spend time with or speak to on occasion. They are important relationships and you enjoy their company, but they are not the ones you reach out to when you need motivation, validation, or advice. Life gets busy and time is limited. It's not possible to be in constant contact with all those people in our lives.

These are valuable relationships and should be nurtured but may not be those that you are in contact with on a regular basis. Although these relationships may not have as much impact on your mindset as those in your inner circle, they should still be positive and encouraging relationships.

People come into our life for a reason, season, or lifetime. Keeping this in perspective helps with understanding our relationships and may lessen the hurt that may come when a relationship ends. Some relationships will end without our understanding of why they ended. Some people will walk in and out of our life or may be taken away from you by illness or death. Some people come into our life to teach us something about ourselves and provide us with an opportunity for growth. Some may come into our life to help us through a difficult time or transition period. Yet others may be in our life to walk alongside us on our journey for a lifetime. Keeping all this in perspective helps to keep us focused on the goodness in our relationships and the purpose in all who come into our life.

A couple years after my separation and months after my divorce was final, I entered the dating world. After a twenty-year marriage and having been out of the dating scene for roughly twenty four years, I quickly found out that a lot had changed. Dating in your forties is different than dating in your late teens and early twenties. You can really learn a lot about yourself when re-entering the dating world. Meeting guys at various ends of the spectrum can be challenging.

There are the ones who desperately want to be in a committed relationship and fall madly in love after date number two, and those that run the instant it may feel like it's becoming an actual relationship. From each man I have dated, whether it be one date or months of dating, I learned more about myself. I've learned what I want in a committed relationship as well as the characteristics I don't want. There have been sincere and honest men, some who fear commitment and can't let go of their past, and others who have no regard for others' feelings.

Believing that everyone has a purpose in our life adds value to each relationship. A clear mindset allows you to take in the lessons learned and let go of any hurt allowing you to maintain clarity. When you have a purpose and know your vision, your relationships have more depth and meaning. It becomes easier to let go of those that are unhealthy or distracting.

There have been too many times I've seen people pulled away from their dreams by the influence of others. Sometimes parents with the best of intentions can steer their children away from their dream because it doesn't make sense to them. As a parent, it's important to provide a safe environment for your children to grow. Providing support and unconditional love allows them to build confidence in themselves. There is nothing more gratifying as a parent than to watch your children live successful and happy lives. Fortunately, both my parents were encouraging and supportive. I knew when there was disapproval but never felt like a failure in their eyes.

My father often validated me by telling me how proud he was of the person I had become. He was elated when I graduated from my master's program and always made it a point to tell me how proud he was of the mother I am to my two boys.

As a mother, it's a privilege to watch my adult children living their lives with success and passion. They are following their dreams and truly engaging in life, through adventures and taking chances. Parenting is not always easy but keeping the perspective that you are guiding these young people to be productive adults helps keep you focused.

Take an inventory of who you are surrounding yourself with. Who is getting the most of your time and energy? Be aware of your energy level and how you feel around them. Make sure they are encouraging, supportive and reciprocal relationships.

Relationships

We have all been designed for relationships and are meant to share our lives with others. Being respectful, kind and loving towards others is our responsibility. Setting limits is necessary to nurture our own inner thoughts, emotions, and energy. A clear mindset allows us to build empathy for others. Be aware of your influence on those around you. We may not always know who is watching or listening to us. Presenting yourself in a positive and encouraging way will have a great impact on others.

Bringing it all Together

"As a child I felt invincible and then life happened. I loved and lost, failed and triumphed, laughed and cried. Felt doubt and experienced pain. I've known peace and fear. I have lived life and believe I AM invincible."

There are so many facets to developing a healthy, positive and clear mindset. Although our goals may differ, we all should be living the life we have been created to live. Realizing your purpose and gaining clear focus, are the catalyst to positive change. Clearing out the negative and releasing the false statements that clutter our minds are important in achieving a mindset that drives us to live a fulfilling life.

It is important to be aware of the message of your internal voice. The words you tell yourself daily have a direct impact on your mindset. I can ask a client what they believe their weaknesses are, and they will quickly answer. However, when I ask them their strengths, there is often hesitation, and the list of strengths is much less than their weaknesses. As you begin to focus on the positive, it becomes easier to catch the negative talk going on in your head. Begin to stop yourself and switch the negative thoughts and words to positive ones. Write a positive statement or word on a piece of paper and have it on your nightstand, in your car, and on your bathroom mirror. Put it in your phone and set a reminder throughout the day to see it. Begin internalizing your strengths and positive self-statements.

Learn to laugh at yourself and your mistakes. A sense of humor will do wonders for your mindset and your life. Laughter stimulates the brain as it increases endorphins and sends dopamine to the brain, which triggers the pleasure and reward system. It is true that laughter is the best medicine. Your energy becomes lighter and it attracts positive energy. Laughter is contagious and can help brighten someone's day. Without laughter and a sense of humor, life would be boring. I couldn't survive in my family without a sense of humor. There is a lot of love in my family, but equally as much sarcasm. Some of my sons' fondest memories of my dad was his quirky sense of humor. Many people have shared that my laugh has brightened their mood.

Laughter relieves stress and pain. Sometimes the only way to move past a difficult time is to find laughter in the situation. In a relationship, laughing can decrease the intensity of an argument. It's also a great way to exercise your abs. I use humor with my clients, when appropriate, and it often helps them gain a lighter perspective on things that may be troubling them. Allow yourself to find laughter in each day and learn to laugh at your mistakes.

As you focus on transforming your mind, you want to increase your overall health and wellness. The abundance of research on exercise and its impact on focus and clarity proves the direct link to mindset and health. A year ago, I completed my first half marathon. The process of training was just as much mental as it was physical. I was already focused on healthy eating and exercise but having the goal of the half marathon added a different perspective to my life. The journey of training and completing this became a clearing and resetting of my mindset. In fact, each mile of the 13.1 miles, I consciously released various emotions that were stored in my mind. It was the most invigorating feeling I've ever felt when I crossed that finish line. Never would I have thought I could complete such a task. You don't have to run a half marathon, but I realized how impactful physical activity and self-care has on our mindset. A simple ten-minute walk is enough to cause a positive shift both physically and mentally.

In addition to exercise, what you use to fuel your body also fuels your mind. Nutrition is another factor that impacts clarity. Brain fog blocks clear thinking and focus

Bringing it all Together

and is caused by lack of sleep, stress, and poor nutrition. Proper nutrition affects our energy, mood and motivation as well.

We are each unique physiologically, which means our nutritional needs vary. Learn to pay attention to your body, get regular check-ups and discuss your nutrition with your doctor. There are a variety of nutrition experts out there. Reach out and educate yourself on what is best for your specific needs. Dr. Kirby Thompson, owner of Wildflower Wellness, LLC, offers this perspective on health and mindset: "As a Naturopathic physician and licensed Acupuncturist, I constantly see the mind-body connection. The body and how we treat it, what we put into it and expose it to can affect the mind: thought processes, emotions, feelings, etc. This can be seen with people that have pain, weight gain, fatigue and other symptoms when going through stressful life events. The body affects the mind with the foods we eat. Eating processed and convenient foods that contain additives which can cause the body to secrete inflammatory chemicals, hormones and can precipitate imbalances which may lead to anxieties, depression, insomnia, brain fog and other mental and emotional symptoms. Once people begin to eat healthier foods they notice a positive shift in emotional states, less mood swings and they start feeling more clarity and focus."

Equally important is feeding our soul. As stated throughout this book, our mind, body, heart and soul are intertwined. Each part must be nurtured and cared for as one affects another. As we develop a grateful, forgiving, and caring mindset, we are directly nurturing our soul. As you spend time being still, you allow your soul to rest. Starting and ending your day focused on gratitude, as in priming your mind also feeds your soul with positive energy. Focusing your mind on your purpose and the positive aspects of life ignites your passion and pleases your soul. Prayer or meditation are effective ways to listen and feel connected to our soul.

Another way to nurture not only your soul but your heart and mind is by giving back to others. There are many ways to give and it doesn't have to be monetary. You may give your time, talents or gifts. Spend time with someone you may know is alone, provide food for a family in need, help with household repairs or donate clothes, books or toys. Join a local charity as a volunteer or participate in fundraisers. Go on a mission trip with your church or participate in activities that improve your community. It's not what we receive but what we give that is most rewarding. When you begin living life with purpose and intent, you can achieve your dreams. It takes motivation, belief in yourself and your purpose, a vision and faith to live an abundant and fulfilling life. What is the benefit of abundance without generosity? Furthermore, sharing your time, talents and generosity with others is the truth of what life is all about. Just as we are all created with inner passion and purpose, we are meant to share our gifts with others. It is in sharing that we are truly fulfilled.

My last piece of advice to you is to be true to yourself! Be real, authentic and genuine. You will begin to exude a positive energy and happiness that others will feel, see and begin to want to know your secret. You'll build confidence as you release your fears and learn growth and success happen outside your comfort zone. Declare your purpose and your vision and you'll begin realizing it. Clear your mind of the clutter, doubt and negativity. We may not be able to control all our circumstances nor predict the obstacles we will encounter on our journey. However, we do have control over our perceptions, thoughts and how we express our emotions. We can tackle anything life hands us, and we have the ability to turn every obstacle into a triumph, every failure into success, and every relationship into a lesson and valuable asset in our lives. Nothing is by chance and we will not face anything that we cannot grow through. Face the struggles, losses, traumas and failures: process them and let them go. Look for the silver lining and incorporate it into your being.

The personal stories I have shared about my life may not be all that unique but are simply a snapshot of the struggles I have experienced and have overcome. They are the experiences I have faced that have enriched my empathy for others which allows me to live out my purpose in helping others in a much richer and more compassionate way. They have allowed me to embrace life which a deep passion and put value in each day and experience. It is my hope that all of you can turn your struggles into your strengths, to forgive and start living in the present. Additionally, that you may find gratitude in all your experiences, circumstances and relationships. Most of all that you take time each day to be still and listen. Listen to your inner voice: for it is that voice that connects your mind, body, heart and soul. The voice that allows you to know your purpose and ignite your passion.

Clarity and purpose are sustained when you get up, get out and LIVE! You can and will achieve your dreams when you believe in yourself and your purpose and develop the gift of perseverance. The key to a life of abundance, success and fulfillment is to live each day with passion, laugh often and love yourself and others with the deepest part of your soul.

If you would like to contact me for further guidance, insights, coaching, or speaking engagements: I can be reached at the following email: wendie@wendielloyd.com. Follow me on Facebook or Instagram @wendie_lloyd. For updates on events and other opportunities to connect.

PEACE, LOVE and SUCCESS!

Wendie

Made in the USA
Columbia, SC
23 March 2018